BUNBURY TAI

Story by David English   Pictures by Jan B

Introduced by Ian Botham

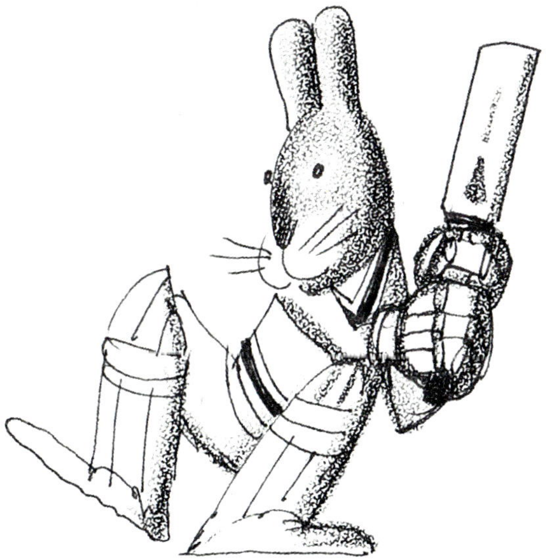

ARTHUR BARKER LIMITED
A SUBSIDIARY OF WEIDENFELD (PUBLISHERS) LIMITED

For Ian, the one and only 'Beefy'.

Published in Great Britain by
Arthur Barker Limited
91 Clapham High Street
London SW4 7TA

ISBN 0 213 16934 7

Printed in Italy

Introduction by Ian Botham

David English is a great pal of mine who has always had a lot of BUNNY!

Well, forget Guy the Gorilla for the moment and say hello to
Ian Buntham, all-rounder extraordinaire,
and let me introduce you to this fascinating contest, Bunbury Tails,
illustrated beautifully by Jan Brychta.

I hope you enjoy it as much as I have.

Ian Botham
Somerset CCC and England

Deep in the forest outside the village of Bunbury, the bunnies were enjoying the warm English summer.

As young Milbun and Edbuns played with their friends, they heard the distant pitter-patter of applause.

Following the sound, they came across the village green and what they saw made them stop in their tracks.

‘Quick, hide in the bushes!’ whispered Edbuns. ‘What are they doing?’ enquired Milbun, peering through the leaves.

Together, the two bunnies watched the men in white throwing the ball, hitting it and then chasing it to all parts of the green.

‘They must be mad hatters to run around like that in this weather,’ exclaimed the bunnies.

Edbuns and Milbun were so excited that they scampered back to Sleepy Time Hollow to tell their friends of their new discovery.

'There are two sides: one out in the field and one in. Each man that's in the side that's in goes out and when he's out he comes in and the next man goes in until he's out. When they are all out the side that's out comes in and the side that's been in goes out and tries to get those coming in out. Sometimes you get men still in and not out. When both sides have been in and out including the not outs, that's the end of the game. Howzat!' panted Edbuns.

'Well, if you can follow that, you're a better bunny than I am,' smiled Holbun, the wise old rabbit. 'But it sounds like a lot of fun, so let's give it a go! Everyone must help make the equipment.'

So the young bunnies nibbled away furiously at the willow trees and made the bats and the wickets . . . while their mothers and grannies knitted and designed the clothes, carefully following Edbuns' and Milbun's descriptions.

The equipment was finally ready – it looked fantastic!

When the church clock struck midnight and the humans had been in bed for some hours, the bunnies started a tough training session. One particular bunny shone above the others. He was Ian Buntham, a strong hitter and fast bowler who could swing the ball in all directions.

The Bunbury CC First Eleven

Ian Buntham
Captain

Robin Jackrabbit
Fast bowler

Dennis Lettuce
Fast bowler – burrowed from Australia

Philip Edbuns
Left-arm spinney bowler

John Emberbunny
Off-break and long hop specialist

Goldenhare Gower
Graceful left-handed batsman

Bob Tailer
Vice-captain and wicketkeeper

Rodney Munch
Aussie wicketkeeper and batsman

Viv Radish
West Indies super bunny batsman

Colin Milbun
Opening batsman

Graham Burrow
Batsman and master fielder

Young Rajbun
Twelfth man – enthusiastic all-bounder

Giant

‘Now we’re ready,’ said Holbun. ‘Let’s play our first game next Saturday night.’

When Saturday night came the moon beamed brightly in a star-filled sky and the bunnies marched out proudly in their smart new clothes.

‘There’s only one problem,’ said Milbun. ‘There seems to be something missing.’

‘I know what it is,’ cried skipper Buntham. ‘We have no hop-position!’

This announcement brought giggles from the bushes.

‘Who’s that laughing?’ said Graham. ‘Quick, Bob, it’s coming from over there!’

To his surprise, Bob Tailer found three cats laughing their heads off.

‘What’s your name?’ said Bob to their leader.

‘Geoff . . . Geoff Boycat,’ replied the peeping-tom.

‘Well, instead of laughing, why don’t you come and play?’ asked Viv.

This seemed a good idea, so off drove the cats in their Purr-geot to their home in nearby Whiskertown, eager to tell their friends of the bunnies' challenge.

'Rally round, all you kitties, we are going to play cricket against Bunbury in the first Bunson and Hedges, Cat West Final next Friday!' shouted Geoff. 'And we need the strongest side possible!'

'Cricket! That's a rare kettle of fish. How do we get a team by Friday? The Cat West Final could become our cat-as-trophy!' shouted the kitties.

Undeterred, Boycat recruited his team by day and by night.

Whiskertown had not seen such hectic activity since the milk strike back in 1977.

Sitting on his cat-a-log, watching the training, was Whiskertown's eldest statesman and chief librarian, Chairman Miaow, pondering over his little red book.

After a long paws, he purred with pleasure and announced the following team.

The Whiskertown CC First Eleven

Geoff Boycat
Captain and opening batsman

Imran Kitten
Pakistani all-rounder

Jeff Thomcat
Australian fast bowler

Pat Pocat
Spin bowler

Vencat
Indian batsman

Pussycat Willis
Vice-captain and opening fast bowler

Paul Downcat
Wicketkeeper

Mike Catting
Batsman and medium-fast bowler

Chris Tabby-Ray
Batsman

Sunil Gavaskat
Indian super batsman

Graham Pooch
In the doghouse – Barking CC

Peter Purrfit
Twelfth man

The Whiskertown team spent the next few days and nights practising and also swotting up on the finer points of the game in Miaow's library.

'If we are to beat Bunbury, we must have a good all-round knowledge of the laws of cricket,' lectured Miaow.

'Phew,' panted an exhausted Imran. 'I haven't had a cat-nap all week!'

In their final trial game, big black clouds started to scud across the sky, hiding the moon and leaving the ground in darkness.

'What can we do?' cried the cats, desperately trying to see where they were going.

'Don't worry,' smiled Geoff. 'I've got an idea. Just leave it to our supporters and friends. OK lads, turn it on!'

High above, in a tree, an owl put his head to one side and laughed: 'Owlzat . . . cats' eyes to the rescue!' Dozens of cats' eyes beamed, illuminating the ground.

Meanwhile, back in Sleepy Time Hollow, disaster had struck the bunnies. Goldenhare Gower had been hit by a long hop during practice and would not be fit for the big game.

'Who can we pick, Skipper?' exclaimed the bunnies.

'How about me?' enquired Rajbun. All eyes turned to the little bunny.

'You're far too young,' laughed the others.

'I don't know,' pondered Buntham. 'We will have to see.'

Friday morning finally dawned, and the spectators arrived at the village green to watch the Cat West Final. Umpires Bill Alley-Cat and Dickie Purred drove up in their hutchback.

Honest Buck, the turf accountant, was having a field day: 'Will they do it? Place your bets. Your chance to make a few bob.'

All around the green, there was a buzz of excitement as Whiskertown won the toss and elected to bat.

It was a fierce contest between the fast bowling of Dennis Lettuce and Ian Buntham and the big hitting of Imran Kitten and Mike Catting.

'Lettuce looks like John McEnroe in that headband,' chortled the spectators, quietly getting merry on carrot juice.

'No sweat, man,' murmured Dennis as he pounded in to bowl. Lettuce let go of the delivery. Catting took a mighty swing, sending the ball spiralling into the sky. All the spectators held their breaths as it began its descent.

'Yours, Raj,' shouted Buntham. 'It's your ball!'

Sure enough, the little bunny was in position but, alas, he lost sight of it in the sun. It came crashing down on his turbanned head, knocking him out.

'Oh no!' gasped the Bunbury supporters as Rajbun was carried off the ground on a stretcher. 'Poor lad, now we're one short!'

So absorbed were the spectators in the battle on the field, they didn't notice the sky going dark. Suddenly the heavens opened and it rained cats and dogs.

Most of the players scurried into the pavilion for cover.

When the shower had passed, Dickie Purred marched out with his meter to check the light.

'OK, I adjudi-cat that play can resume in five minutes.' The spin-twins of Edbuns and Emberbunny weaved their magic as the sun dried out the pitch.

Whiskertown finally made 176 runs with Boycat top scorer on 67.

Old Holbun and Chairman Miaow sat together eating their tea.

'Purr-fect! I think we've got enough runs to win,' smiled a confident Miaow, 'especially as you're a man short.'

'That's enough of that, Old Bunny,' laughed Holbun. 'It's our turn now!'

Bunbury started briskly with an opening stand of 65 between Graham Burrow and Colin Milbun.

The pace bowling of Pussycat Willis and Jeff Thomcat then took its toll. Willis completed the cat-trick in taking the wickets of Rodney Munch, Bob Tailer and Robin Jackrabbit. Finally the two Bunbury idols, Radish and Buntham were left at the wicket to save the match.

Steadily, Radish and Buntham chipped away at the total, stopping for some welcome lettuce and milk brought on by their twelfth man.

'What's the news on young Raj?' panted Buntham.

'Sorry, Skip, I'm afraid he's still seeing stars.'

When the game restarted, Viv despatched the ball in every direction in true calypso fashion before being run out by a great throw from Tabby-Ray. He had scored 52 and left the field to tumultuous applause.

Skipper Buntham was then joined by Edbuns who was immediately bowled for a golden duck. Dennis Lettuce added a few runs in typically robust fashion before being caught superbly by wicketkeeper Downcat.

Ten to win and Buntham had run out of partners. The cool cats went wild.

Surely, it had to be the end for Bunbury with their eleventh man still out for the count. Then, just as the umpires went to remove the bails and pronounce a Whiskertown win, there was a stunned silence all around the ground.

There . . . tottering on the pavilion steps, was young Rajbun, clutching his bat, his head heavily bandaged around his turban.

Out wobbled the little rabbit, not quite sure in which direction the wicket lay.

'Over here!' yelled Buntham. 'Good lad, Raj, now just do as I say.'

High up in the tree, the Bunbury Broadcasting Corporation was commentating at fever pitch. 'Forgive us for rabbitting on, but I can't recall this happening since Cowdrey batted one-handed against the West Indies in 1963!' shrieked Richie Bunaud and Bunny Johnston into their microphones. 'What a test of courage for this youngster.'

BUNBURY

Imran galloped up to the wicket, Buntham leapt out and drove the ball clear over the pavilion for six. The crowd went mad. So did Imran. Four to win. The next ball whistled around the skipper's ears. Calmly he stood back and hooked it. Was it a boundary? No! Gavaskat cut it off for three. One run to win and little Rajbun to face the bowling. The crowd was hushed.

In came Imran. It was a fearsome bouncer. The ball rapped Rajbun's bat handle, and went zooming through the slips for four.

Bunbury had won the game. The crowd were beside themselves with joy as Ian Buntham chaired young Rajbun off the field.

As Geoff Boycat presented the fourteen carrot trophy to Buntham, the Bunbury skipper smiled: 'Well played Raj. You can keep this, you deserve it!'

The lines at the Whiskertown British Telecat Exchange were jammed. 'You must come and play us. Send your best players!' enthused the operator.

That night young Rajbun slept without batting an eyelid. His trophy on the mantelpiece and his trusty bat by his side, he fell into a happy dream.

Today. . .Bunbury. Tomorrow. . .Lord's and the rest of the world!